Nectar is a sweet, sugary liquid.
The bee laps up the nectar with
its long tongue.

tongue   nectar

It carries away the nectar in a
honey sac inside its body.

7

While the bee is drinking nectar, pollen grains from the flower stick to its furry body and legs.

pollen on body

pollen basket

The bee puts the pollen into little pockets on its legs, called pollen baskets. You can see them in the picture.

When the bee moves on, some of the pollen on its body rubs off on the new flower.
This is called pollination.

What is pollination?

When a plant has been pollinated, it can make seeds that will grow into new plants.

11

Insects have helped to pollinate flowers for millions of years.

Insects like nectar, but they also like the flowers' strong smells and bright colours.

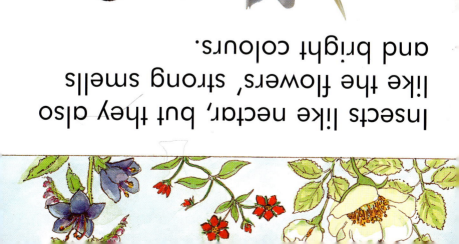

Many flowers have lines or bright spots on their petals that lead to the middle of the flower.

These show bees and other insects where the nectar is.

When a bee's honey sac is full of nectar, it flies back to its nest.

Some bees nest in trees or rocky cracks. Others nest in wooden hives.

How many flowers does a bee visit?

A bee visits hundreds of flowers. It takes 60 sacs of nectar to make a thimbleful of honey.

queen

drone

In a nest of honeybees, there are thousands of bees and one queen bee.

What does she do?

The queen bee lays the eggs. In each nest there are a few male bees, called drones. They mate with the queen bee.

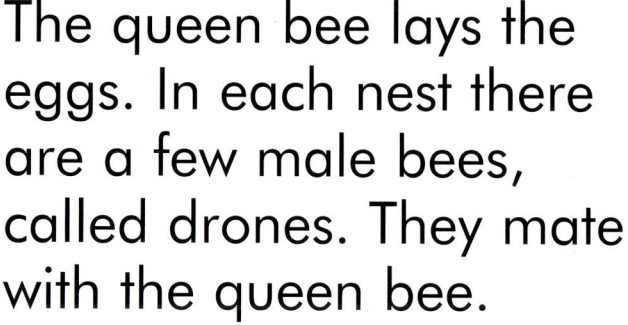

16

eggs

workers

The rest of the bees are female worker bees. They clean the nest, feed the young and make honey.

17

The nest contains wax combs, made up of lots of little cells where the queen bee lays her eggs. Each egg hatches into a larva. Each cell has a wax lid.

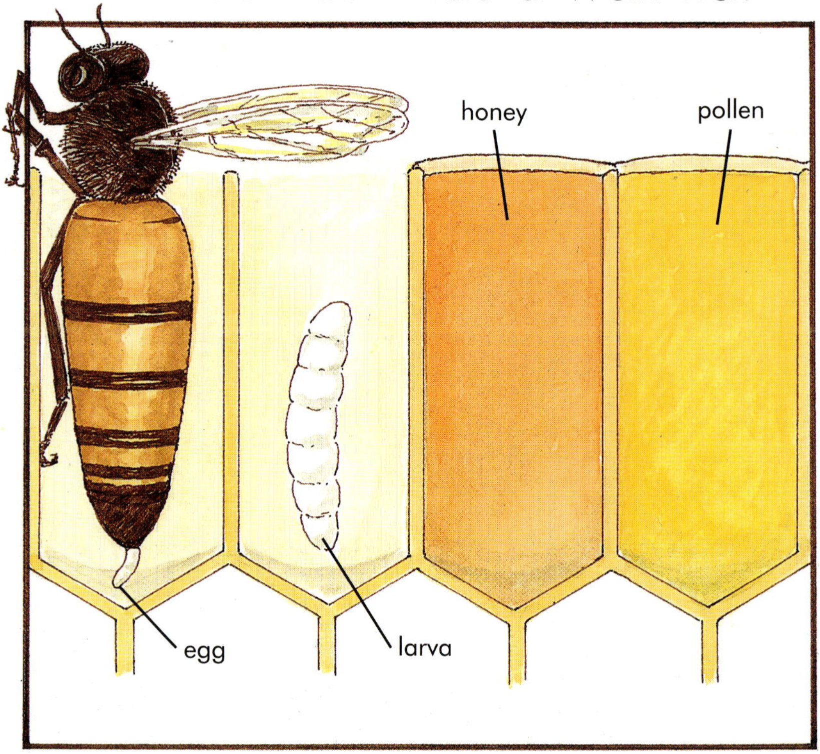

honey

pollen

egg

larva

Honey and pollen are also kept in the comb. This is food for the bees and larvae.

People keep bees in hives to collect their honey. The hive is a bit like a nest.

A hive has different rooms, or chambers, where the bees make combs. The top chamber is for honeycombs.

top chamber

brood chamber

The queen bee lives in the brood chamber. She lays her eggs in combs.

A grid stops the queen bee getting into the top chamber to lay eggs.

The beekeeper collects the honeycombs from the top chamber.

To make the honey, a bee first brings the nectar up from its honey sac back into its mouth. It gives the nectar to a worker bee, which swallows it into its 'honey stomach'.

Does the worker bee make the honey?

There, the nectar is changed into watery honey. The worker bee brings the honey back up into its mouth.

Nurse bees feed the honey to the larvae. Each larva needs 1000 meals a day!

23

The bees eat left-over honey and pollen in the winter, when there are not many flowers.

When beekeepers take honeycomb from hives, they give the bees sugar to feed on instead.

Animals like this bear take honey from nests and hives, too.

A bear's thick furry coat keeps it safe from stings.

Some animals, including toads, spiders and dragonflies, actually eat bees. If a bee uses its sting, it dies.

Bees use two dances to 'talk'
to each other.

When a bees does the 'round
dance', it is telling the other
bees that food is no more than
25 metres away.

The 'waggle dance' tells the other bees that food is further away and shows them which way to fly.

hive

food

sun

27

A nest of bees can make nearly a kilo of honey in a day.

Beekeepers wear special clothes so that the bees can't sting them.

28

The honeycombs are put into
a machine called an extractor.
The machine takes the honey
out of the comb. The honey is
put into jars.

Mmmm, I like honey!

Answers:
1 Putting honey in the comb 2 Putting a wax lid on the cells 3 Flying back to the hive with full pollen baskets 4 Giving nectar to another bee 5 Feeding larvae
6 Dancing 7 Queen bee laying eggs

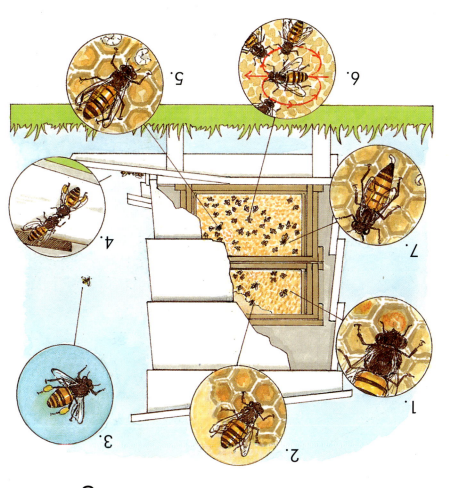

This is a picture of the inside of a hive. Can you work out what all the bees are doing?

Index

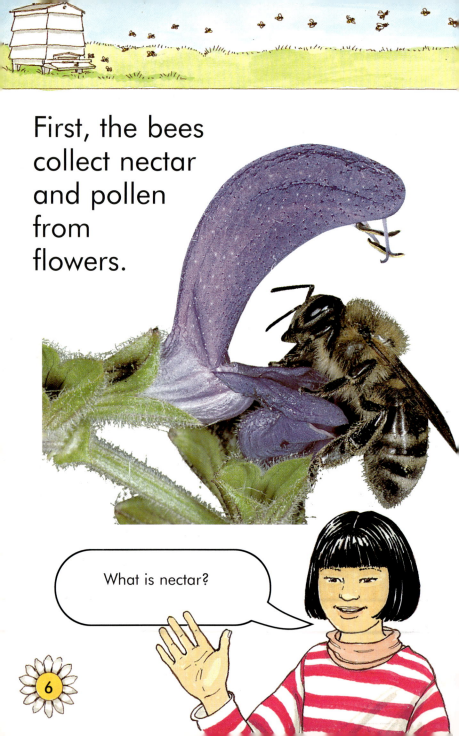

First, the bees collect nectar and pollen from flowers.

What is nectar?

6

Let's find out how
bees make honey
from flowers.

Published by Evans Brothers Limited
2A Portman Mansions
Chiltern Street
London, W1U 6NR

First published in this edition 2005

Printed in China by W KT Co., Ltd.

ISBN 0 237 52933 5

ACKNOWLEDGEMENTS
Planning and production by The Creative Publishing Company
Edited by Patience Coster
Designed by Ian Winton

For permission to reproduce copyright material, the author and publishers
gratefully acknowledge the following:
Biofotos: cover (top left), pages 5 (bottom), 12 (Heather Angel), 19 (Andrew Henley);
Bruce Coleman: cover (top right) and 15 (Kim Taylor), pages 6 (Dr Frieder Sauer), 10, 28
(George McCarthy); Natural Science Photos: pages 5 (top) (T.A. Moss), 9 (Jeremy Burgess),
14 (Steve Downer), 21, 23 (Richard Revels); Oxford Scientific Films: cover (main picture),
pages 13 (Scott Camazine), 16-17, 22 (David Thompson), 24 (Philippe Henry).

How Bees Make Honey

Helena Ramsay

Illustrated by Jenny Mumford

Evans